Foundations for a Sustainable & Prosperous World

~ Matthew Martin

along with VisionaryPolitics.net

Acknowledgments to the 2002 Earth Charter
and the 1972 UN Declaration on Our Human Environment

Contents

**Human Rights
& Social Fairness**   5

**Globally Cooperative
& Generous Governments**   15

**Environmentally Responsible
Governments & Economies**   33

**Teaching Social
& Ecological Values**   57

**The Goals & Activities
of the United Nations**   63

**24 Sustainable
Development Goals**   71

Human Rights
& Social Fairness

10 Kinds of Human Rights

1. **Security** – ensure human security and safety for everyone, free from threats of violence and forced enslavement.

2. **Survival** – ensure healthy food, clean water, and adequate shelter for everyone.

3. **Health** – ensure health care and health safety for everyone.

4. **Education** – ensure the availability of a basic education and life-skills for everyone.

5. **Freedom** – ensure freedom of speech, beliefs, religion, lifestyle, choices, artistic creations, and group gatherings; as long as this is not judicially judged as harmful to other people or to a sustainable & unpolluted natural environment.

6. **Justice** – ensure equal justice and fair civil laws for everyone, without systemic prejudice, racism, sexism, and without economic or social oppression.

7. **Economic Opportunities** – ensure non-discriminating economic opportunities for everyone – for securing personal and family survival, along with increased opportunities for economic advancement.

8. **Democratic Participation** – ensure equal opportunity to participate in national and community decisions, with equal access to voting and minority-inclusive representation.

9. **Communication** – ensure freedom in all inter-social communication, media, news, and information-access; without government surveillance violating people's rights of privacy, though with reasonable restrictions on inciting violence, excessive media violence, and sexual or violent content intended for children.

10. **Special Protections** – ensure the safety and equal rights of physically and economically vulnerable persons, such as: women & children, elderly & disabled, homeless & poor, farmers & laborers, minorities & indigenous, migrants & refugees, imprisoned & politically detained.

Ensure Basic Human Needs

– Ensure a basic economic security for human survival.

– Ensure access to nutritious food, clean water, adequate sanitation, protective shelter, and a safe & healthy environment.

– Increase access to healthcare, medicines, counseling, maternity needs and family planning.

Protect Human Safety
human safety is a human right

– Ensure a safe shelter and residence for all people.

– Provide a safe refuge in another area or country, in cases of emergency or dangerous conflicts.

– Protect the safety of women, children, and all socially vulnerable persons.

– Reduce and finally end all armed conflicts and weaponized threats.

– Reduce and finally end all domestic and societal violence.

– Maintain a healthy natural environment for all communities.

Equal & Fair Justice

equal & fair justice is a civil right

– Governments should have a fair and equal justice system, to resolve conflicts and decide a fair and just reparation for any evident harms to others, to other's property, or to the common environment.

– Equal laws for everyone in a nation or community, without discrimination.

– No physical violence against others, nor threats of violence, nor encouragement of violence.

– No harm to or depletion of the common environment or public resources, without financial compensation.

– Fair procedural processes to determine guilt, and determine a fair recompense, reparation, or punishment if judged to be guilty.

– No detainment without reason, no assumptions of guilt without proof, no secret trials, no slavery, no torture, and no physical threats.

– An equitable compensation for a person's labor, invention, or contribution to society.

Equal Freedoms

All people have a human right
to the following freedoms,
without prejudice or discrimination
towards any gender, race,
ethnic, religious or cultural groups,
nor towards any minority political affiliations.

All people should have the freedom of:

- beliefs & opinions

- speech & creative expression

- religious & cultural practices

- personal privacy & chosen lifestyle

- social & political affiliation

- peaceful assembly & political dissent

- public discussion & uncensored debate

Educational Opportunities

– Increase everyone's access to education, skills-learning and technical know-how.

– Promote educational contributions from all sciences, arts, and philosophies.

– Provide youth and all ages with the knowledge and skills needed to be more self-reliant and self-responsible, to solve problems and help people, to participate in governing decisions, and to improve society and the world.

– Provide extra educational help for those with learning difficulties.

Opportunities to Participate in Government

– Every adult has the right to speak about and participate in their local and national government, without any discrimination.

– Promote more inclusive participation and diversity representation in government agencies and governing decisions.

– Promote more participation of women as decision makers and leaders, in all aspects of government, economics, health, and education.

– Encourage and enable younger adults to participate more in governing discussions, decisions and plans for the future.

– Increase opportunities for grassroots democracy, residential initiatives and referendums, voting and diversity-proportional representation.

– Increase transparency and accountability in government decisions & policies, and in any proposed community or economic development plans.

– Eliminate government corruption, bribery, and excessive influence from large corporations, investment coalitions and industries.

Economic Rights

– Everyone has a human right to a basic economic security, including sufficient food, clean water, adequate shelter, sanitation and healthcare.

– Guaranteed care for all children, elderly, and disabled persons.

– Job opportunities for everyone, with labor rights, safe workplaces and fair equitable pay.

– Equal access to educational and skills-learning opportunities.

– Business opportunities (with helpful capital-loans), and fair market trade.

– Government subsidies or low-interest loans to need-targeted communities, for starting new businesses or for employing any of the local unemployed, in jobs that benefit the community in some way, either in the social sphere of the community or in the caretaking of the surrounding ecosystems of that region.

Rights of Ownership

– The right to own personal property or a business.

– The right to buy or trade goods, services, property or investments.

– The right to protect the ownership of one's own artistic creations, writings and inventions.

– The rights of indigenous people to their sacred lands, natural resources, and cultural lifestyles.

– The right of communities to socially-determine the degree of public land and industries, within their living & work areas.

– The right to not be controlled or exploited by self-serving economic powers.

Globally Cooperative & Generous Governments

Global Dialogue and Collaboration

– Strengthen the United Nations to be a global arena and global-leading organization, collaboratively working for a healthy and sustainable global environment, healthy global ecosystems, human health, human rights, human safety, and greater prosperity for all people.

– Increase the inclusiveness and diversity of group representation in the global decision-making and agreements of the United Nations.

– Foster collaborative, constructive and transparent dialogue involving representatives of national governments, international economic and social institutions, civil society groups and world academia, regarding current global problems and how to best solve them.

– Collaboratively work to establish international agreements on: environmental and ecological protections, human rights and civil freedoms, social justice and economic security, peace and human security, improving health and education, sustainable development and fair trade, and economic assistance to poorer communities.

– Encourage more citizen dialogue & discussion in social media and world news about important global issues, international policies and agreements, and also encourage grassroots and civil society organizations to help solve global problems.

– Establish independent global monitoring and transparent communication of how international laws and agreements are being implemented by sovereign nations.

– Establish global and national institutions to help build cooperation (or 'partnership') between governments and private-capital corporations, banks & investment firms; to collaboratively achieve global environmental & climate goals, and to coordinate international economic assistance to poorer and less developed nations.

International Peace and Human Safety

– Acknowledge that human safety (from violence, threats of violence, and armed conflicts) is a Human Right.

– Acknowledge that international and regional cooperation (for solving common global problems and for economic trade) helps achieve global and regional peace.

– Establish an effective United Nations Peacekeeping Force, along with peacebuilding offices and projects.

– Establish United Nations Conflict-mediation Teams, to help conflicting nations or tribal groups agree on a peaceful compromising resolution.

– Encourage international and civil society Peacebuilding Projects throughout the world, with local participation, including mediation assistance in conflict reconciliation and restorative justice.

– Revise the UN Security Council to be effective in fulfilling its intended function, which is to strengthen peace and security in the world, through cooperative and transparent dialogue, conflict resolution, and international peace agreements.

– Increase international peace diplomacy, peace treaties, and international collaboration projects; rather than escalating threats, conflicts and wars.

– All nations should mutually agree to significantly disarm and reduce their militaries, while maintaining only a non-provocative and non-threatening defense for their national security.

– Eliminate all weapons of mass destruction; including nuclear, biological, and chemical weapons.

– Ban all outer-space weapons, and ensure that all orbital instruments and materials are used only for peaceful and scientific purposes.

Protect Human Security and Reduce Violence

– Establish International Peace through dialogue, negotiation, agreements, and consensus-building.

– Establish Peace Agreements and International Laws that will ensure an end to all tribal, racial, and inter-national aggression.

– Establish reliable security and protections for women, children, the elderly, disabled, displaced, refugees and immigrants.

– Establish equal participation in security decisions with proportional gender and race representation in all security and human rights decision-making.

– Establish norms and best-practices for conflict prevention, crisis management, peaceful settlement of disputes, and post-conflict peace-building.

– Establish international laws to reduce the production and circulation of assault weapons and small arms.

Social & Economic Responsibilities

Governments are encouraged to promote:

– human rights, civil freedoms, social fairness, equal justice, and non-discrimination.

– improving the quality of life and living conditions for everyone.

– wider distribution of economic prosperity and opportunities.

– global and regional fair-trade agreements, with fair and safe labor standards.

– sustainable infrastructure for energy supply, economic transport, and digital communication.

– community and regional self-sufficient & self-resilient economies, with localized energy & food production, accessible water sources, and small-scale technologies.

– globally-cooperative solutions to climate-change; such as reducing carbon-emissions, increasing natural carbon-capture, and developing climate adaptation & resilience in regions and communities.

– strengthen community and agricultural resilience against severe heat, droughts, and floods.

– help decentralized locally-controlled agriculture and food systems, with localized freedom to reproduce agricultural seeds unrestricted by seed-patent laws.

– food and technology supply-chains that are un-manipulated by corporate monopolies and industrial cartels.

– local protections from corporate land-grabbing and corporate controlled land-use.

– business-accountability for harms done to communities, human health, and the natural environment, and establish business-incentives for improving communities, social prosperity, and the natural environment.

International Generosity

Increase basic economic security and improve the living conditions *for all people*

– Ensure that all people have food security, clean drinking water, adequate sanitation, safe shelter, and access to healthcare & emergency services.

– Help improve local-reliant food security and food production in regions, cities and communities.

– Help improve local-regional water security.

– Help improve the quality of life for all people and communities.

– Especially helping migrant and refugee camps, the vulnerable and the underprivileged.

– Emergency Relief from the UN and affiliated groups, for regions affected by severe weather or other natural disasters, and for regions affected by armed conflicts.

Provide Economic Assistance for poorer nations, regions and communities

– Wealthier nations are asked to be more economically generous and helpful to poorer nations, with international assistance and loans for sustainable development, ecological regeneration, and climate solutions.

– Relieve poorer nations of excessive debt problems, by decreasing the interest rates on their loans, and by a generous restructuring of debt.

– Relieve excessive dept by debt-for-nature swaps, which trades debt for more ecological conservation and climate-improving projects or policies.

– Implement effective economic measures to achieve a more equitable distribution of wealth and capital, within nations and among nations.

– Wealthier nations are encouraged to donate 5% of their annual GNP into a World Fund for helping poorer nations and communities become ecologically sustainable, climate helpful, and more economically independent, secure and prosperous. Wealthier nations could ask the wealthiest 5% of individuals, families and corporations to pay most of this national donation to the World Fund, by a progressive income, wealth, property and assets tax.

– Private individuals, groups, businesses, multinational corporations and private-equity investment funds are encouraged to voluntarily give Donations (a fixed $ amount or a percentage of assets) or give other forms of free assistance to nations, regions, communities, or projects of their choice. And governments can 'deduct' these private voluntary donations from those respective wealth or capital-gains taxes.

Provide benefiting employment for all people seeking paid work

– Everyone willing to work should have opportunities for fair-paying work, in order to achieve their economic security or advancement, and for nations to eliminate unemployment and achieve full employment.

– If sufficient job opportunities are not available from the private-sector (capitalism), then the government (national, regional, or local) should organise/initiate 'public services and projects' that are socially-beneficial and/or ecologically-beneficial, in order to employ all people seeking paid work (who could not find work in the private-sector).

– This will effectively eliminate all unemployment of those seeking work, and in addition this will: (a) benefit the local community, the regional infrastructure, and/or the regional ecology; while also (b) eliminate the public need to provide direct economic assistance for the unemployed.

– In order to finance these public services and projects, governments (national, regional, and local) will need to acquire sufficient revenue from progressive taxation on income, wealth and property; and government funding (for poorer nations) can also come from international aide assistance and from international bank or investment loans.

– This government public money can then be used to pay for the social & ecological beneficial services and projects, which includes paying the employed workers and maintaining full employment in every community and city.

– Regions, communities and cities with the most needs and the most unemployed can be specially prioritized and targeted for government grants, subsidies and low-interest (or zero-interest) loans – given to regional and local public services/projects and also to new start-up private businesses or to worker-coop businesses – in order to increase the local employment in community-benefiting jobs that serve social and ecological needs.

Help regions & communities become ecologically sustainable and economically prosperous

– Provide assistance and loans to environmentally & socially beneficial locally-owned small businesses and community-cooperative enterprises.

– Provide helpful international loans to increase local economic self-reliance and prosperity for all communities and regions.

– Provide assistance for increasing regional and local economic independence, along with equitable-fair global trade.

– Provide assistance for localized food production, food independence, and locally-managed food trade markets.

– Provide assistance and incentives for local and regional soil-regenerative farming, for both small private-owned farms and community farming.

– Provide assistance and incentives for the management of community-local and regional ecosystems, including forest, rivers, wetlands and coastal marine management, and the conservation of surrounding wildlands and natural habitats.

– Provide assistance and incentives to increase clean and renewable energy-independence for local communities and cities.

– Provide assistance and incentives for environmentally sustainable infrastructure of energy supply, economic transport, and digital communication.

– Provide extra assistance for migrant and refugee groups to create environmentally and economically sustainable communities, with full employment towards helping the community and the local ecosystem, or working in a profitable trade or business.

Help regions & communities adapt to climate-change and reverse climate-change

– Financially assist poorer nations with low-interest loans and generous aide, in their solutions to global climate-change.

– Financially assist poorer nations in their transition to cleaner energies and fuels.

– Financially assist poorer nations in their projects for increasing natural carbon-capture.

– Financially assist poorer nations in their climate-change preparations, adaptations and resilience.

– Improve local drought and flood resilience, and help agriculture be more climate-resilient.

– With regional and local community engagement, decide on regional climate adaptation strategies and locally-needed climate resilience plans, including disaster risk reduction and emergency response mechanisms.

Provide access to new technologies and technical know-how

– Global open access to the needed knowledge, technologies, and tech-skills for achieving environmentally-sustainability economic progress.

– Financially help poorer nations and communities purchase environmental and life improving technologies, through purchase discounts and no-interest loans.

– Help finance tech-schools and skills-learning, and provide technical support and teachers.

Increase educational opportunities
for everyone and everywhere

– Increase access to basic and extended education.

– Help support schools and job-skills learning.

Increase job and business opportunities
for everyone and everywhere

– Increase community-benefiting job opportunities in each region, city and community.

– Financially assist businesses (private & community-coops) that are environmentally and socially helpful.

Require more financial assistance from wealthy corporations

– Multinational Corporations can contribute 10% of their yearly profits to a World Fund for assisting poorer nations with sustainable development and ecological restoration, and this can be collected each year by progressive taxes on corporation's total capital assets along with their capital gains or windfall-gains for that year.

– Corporations can also be proportionately taxed to support national public services, infrastructure, and socially or ecologically needed projects.

– Investment Companies, Banks and Corporations can be tax-incentivized to invest in and provide low-interest loans to ecological & climate helping community-projects and small businesses.

Environmentally Responsible Governments & Economies

Environmental Goals for Governments

Protect & Restore
ecosystems and biodiversity

Protect & Restore
water & forest ecosystems

Protect Natural Resources
from overuse & depletion

Protect Oceans & Bays
from pollution & overfishing

Reduce Industrial Pollution
of the air, water, and land

Protect Endangered Wildlife
and preserve natural habitats

Establish Conservation Areas,
wildlife & nature reserves

Protect Natural Beauty,
scenic places & landscapes

Reduce Greenhouse Gases
to reduce climate change

Produce & Use
clean & renewable energies

Increase Recycling
of products & materials

Improve Energy-efficiency
in heating & cooling buildings

Increase Forests & Wetlands
for natural carbon-capture

Improve Agricultural Soils
& increase regenerative farming

Environmental Responsibilities
Governments need to advance:

– environmental and climate protection laws.

– ecological and wildlife protection laws.

– regional and locally managed ecological conservation.

– sustainable use of limited natural resources.

– clean non-polluting energy production and industrial processes.

– business accountability for environmental damages or depletion of public natural resources and natural ecosystems, along with financial accountability for industrial and product carbon-emissions.

– business incentives for restoring and improving natural ecosystems, freshwater sources, wildlife habitats, forests, and farm soils, along with financial incentives for reducing carbon-emissions and for carbon-capturing.

Environmental Protections

– Establish national and local environmental protective regulations.

– Protect air quality and the ozone.

– Protect freshwater sources, watersheds, and water quality.

– Protect important natural resources: local, regional, national, and global.

– Protect rare and needed mineral resources.

– Protect the Earth's ecosystems and biodiversity.

– Establish nature and wildland conservation areas.

– Protect endangered wildlife and habitats.

– Protect special areas of natural beauty, scenic landscapes, and recognised sacred lands.

– Ensure that economic development projects are environmentally sustainable and unharmful to local ecosystems or to the global climate.

– Establish climate-solving policies, such as penalizing carbon-emissions and incentivizing carbon-capturing.

– Establish special fines & taxes for climate-harming industrial and energy-production emissions.

– Establish special fines & taxes for all industrial toxic-chemicals leaked or allowed into the air, watersheds, or oceans.

Ecological Conservation and Management

– Provide stewardship and management of the natural environment.

– Protect and restore natural areas, natural ecosystems and wildlife habitats.

– Protect and restore forest, pastoral, and water ecosystems.

– Reverse land and soil degradation, desertification and soil erosion.

– Restore and improve freshwater sources, wetlands, watersheds and aquifers.

– Incentivize local & regional ecological-restoration, tree planting, soil regeneration, watershed and wetlands restoration, with gov funded projects and employment.

– Establish and maintain naturally-regenerative wildlands and nature corridors.

– Establish more biodiversity and wildlife reserves.

- Lawfully protect great wildlife mammals, especially endangered wildlife species, and prevent extinctions; with strong criminal prosecution of offenders.

- Protect wildlife from cruel methods of hunting, trapping, and fishing, that cause extreme, prolonged or avoidable suffering.

- Protect animals from cruelty and avoidable suffering in animal food farming.

- Promote sustainable farming and soil-regeneration, and find ways to complement farmland with natural wildlands and the local ecosystems.

- Promote biodiverse seed conservation.

- Protect and restore coastal marine areas and ocean life.

- Prevent marine eutrophication and ocean acidification.

- Protect ocean-ecosystems and ocean-life by establishing conservation rules and regulations on ocean fishing and other ocean uses.

- Ecologically Manage the use of depleting natural resources from the land and oceans.

- Ecologically Manage the extraction and use of the Earth's non-renewable natural resources, to minimize their depletion and prevent environmental toxic-pollution from their extractive processes.

Protect Oceans & Coastal Waters

– Establish sustainable ocean management, with ocean regulations and protections.

– Protect oceans, bays and marinas from chemical and plastics pollution, untreated sewage and eutrophication, oil spills and fuel spillage.

– Establish marine sanctuaries and protected fish-migration corridors in ecologically vulnerable areas.

– Protect ocean habitats, coral reefs, and important fish colonies.

– Protect oceans & sea-life from bottom-trolling, overfishing, and fish harming by-catch.

– Promote sustainable & ecologically-responsible ocean fishing, with ocean fishing rules.

– Incentivize ecological & health-quality aquaculture.

Stop Pollution
of the air, water, and land

– Acknowledge that environmental health and a non-polluted environment is a human right.

– Prevent all forms of pollution entering into the air, waters, and land.

– Reduce carbon-emissions, air polluting toxins, atmospheric aerosol loading and ozone depletion.

– Reduce health-harming particles polluting the air, from burning fossil fuels for energy production or industrial operations.

– Reduce acid rainfall caused by sulfur dioxide released into the air by coal power plants and other carbon-emitting operations.

– Reduce air pollution from transportation vehicles and heavy machinery.

– Prevent industrial and power-plant toxic chemicals entering into the air and water.

– Prevent all forms of surface and underground water pollution.

– Safely contain and dispose all environmentally toxic substances accumulated from industrial waste and mining processes.

– Prevent container leakage of any toxic, radioactive, or other health-hazardous substances.

– Prevent industrial, pharmaceutical, and cosmetic chemicals from entering into freshwaters, bays and oceans, and into marine-life food chains.

– Prevent toxic metals from industrial & mining processes, such as mercury, lead, chromium, cadmium, asbestos, and arsenic, from entering into the air, rivers, lakes and groundwater aquifers, bays and oceans, and into marine-life food chains.

– Reduce and phase-out toxic health-damaging herbicides and pesticides, that enter into the water to harm fish life, or enter into the air to harm birds and pollinators.

– Prevent agricultural chemical fertilisers, with nitrates and phosphates, entering rivers, lakes, bays and coastal waters.

– Use effective methods for human-waste containment, treatment and disposal; to prevent fecal pathogens entering drinking water, and reduce eutrophication harmful to water ecologies and fish life.

– Prevent industrial operations and power plants from disposing their excess heat into the water ecosystems of rivers, lakes, or bays.

- Prevent excessive nitrogen-rich nutrients from agricultural runoff and human waste entering rivers, lakes, estuaries, coastal waters and marinas, which kills fish and reduces water quality.

- Improve wastewater treatment of human-waste, and penalize eutrophication-causing agricultural methods that use nitrates and phosphates.

- Increase shellfish aquaculture to mitigate eutrophication.

- Prevent pollution of the rivers and oceans with plastic containers, styrofoam, and micro-plastics.

- Encourage consumer recycling of plastics and metals, and rapidly increase recycling industries, local recycling collection centres and effective recycling-separation systems; in order to minimize the amount of plastics & non-degradable products buried in landfills or discarded into rivers and oceans.

- Store non-recyclable waste-products in special landfills or safe underground containment areas.

- Monitor all kinds of air, water, and land pollution, along with the amounts of carbon added to the atmospheric greenhouse.

- Make pollution-emitting industries financially accountable, through special fines or taxes, for the degree of toxic chemicals released into the air, water or land, which harms ecosystems and negatively affects human health.

Reduce & Reverse Climate-change

Reduce carbon-emissions

Reduce global greenhouse gases
by reducing carbon-emissions

Produce and use
clean & renewable energies

Economically incentivize
clean & renewable
energy production & use

Reduce carbon-emissions
from industrial operations

Capture industrial carbon-emissions
and store the carbon underground
or use it to produce new products

Reduce carbon-emissions
from industries & energy-production
by carbon-taxing or by cap-n-trade

Reduce carbon-emissions
from military operations

Reduce carbon-emissions
from transportation vehicles

Economically incentivize
clean & low-emission
transportation vehicles
and industrial machinery

Apply economic incentives
to reduce the consumer use
of carbon-emitting products

Incentivize energy-efficiency
of heating & cooling in buildings

Stop methane leaks from fossil fuel
extraction & from natural gas pipes

Reduce methane emissions
from industrial animal farming
and from landfill bio-waste

Adequately bury landfills and
compost manure & farm waste

Use anaerobic digesters
to make fertilizers & bio-fuels
from farm & landfill waste

Increase natural carbon-capture

Restore and increase
forests & wildlands

Plant more trees & vegetation
in prairies & pastoral lands

Bury or compost
decaying plants & trees

Add more organic material
into agricultural soils

Restore and improve
wetlands & estuaries

Restore and increase
ocean plant life

Incentivize local employment
to plant forests & add compost to soils

Incentivize corporate investments
in natural carbon-capture projects
with tax-breaks or carbon-offset credits

Protect & Increase Forests

– Acknowledge the important social & economic values of forests:

    * the economic resource value

    * the ecological, biodiversity & habitat value

    * the carbon-capture value

    * the aesthetic enjoyment value

– Protect and conserve native forests.

– Create more protected forest reserves.

– Restore previous forests (reforestation),
Plant new forests (afforestation)
Improve current forests.

– Plant more trees in public lands, parks, corridors, neighborhoods, and rurally owned land.

– Create more forest recreation areas, with hiking & biking trails, fishing & boating, camping & dayuse, explorational education, and peaceful retreat groves.

– Large forests should be maintained and managed by the local indigenous people, or by the local community, or by ecologically responsible businesses.

Improve Farming Soils
and their carbon-capture capacity

– Improve the soil texture, humus, microbiome, nutrients, aeration, moisture, and pH balance.

– Add into the soil composted food & plant wastes, aged animal manures, and organic biofertilizers.

– Plant off-season soil-enriching and nitrogen-giving cover crops.

– Use crop rotation and rotate fallow areas.

– Reduce soil compaction and soil erosion.

– Minimize soil tillage, in order to reduce soil erosion, nutrient runoff, loss of soul moisture, and carbon-release into the atmosphere.

– Cover the ground surface between planted crops with mulches and previous crop wastes, in order to improve the soil structure and porosity, increase the soil's organic matter and soil moisture, reduce evaporation and soil erosion, and help fix CO_2 in the soil.

– Intersperse farming land with native plants, fruit & nut trees, and small fast-growth forests, in order to increase moisture and rain in the area, and to decrease flooding, soil erosion and desertification.

– Economically incentivize soil-improving inputs and methods, and economically penalize soil-degrading inputs and methods.

– Farm subsidies and loans should require soil-improving and carbon-capturing methods.

– Economically incentivize the collection of food & plant waste from local urban & rural areas, along with animal manure from local farms & ranches, and build community-scale composting facilities.

Environmentally Responsible Economics

Market-guiding Economic Policies

*Government economic policies
should be guided by
ecological & climate needs*

– Governments need to economically guide free-market activities and private investment towards achieving a healthy and sustainable natural environment.

– Create economic penalties to discourage businesses from harming the public environment, human living conditions, natural ecosystems or the global climate, and to discourage capital investment in business that engage in such harms.

– Create economic incentives to encourage capital investment in businesses and projects that help improve ecological, climate, and human living conditions.

– Governments should apply environmental-guiding economic measures; such as:
 [negatively] -- protective laws, fines, and tax penalties,
 or [positively] -- tax breaks, rebates, subsidies, or contracts.

– Reduce industrial pollution and resource depletion by making industries economically-accountable for their environmental damages and depletion of public natural resources.

- Ensure that all industrial and business activities are economically-accountable for any long-distance & long-term harms to the public environment, to human health, to local communities, to natural ecosystems, resources, or climate.

- Require multinational corporations and international financial organizations to act transparently for the good of environmental and ecological health, climate stabilization, and for improving human living conditions, sustainable communities, cities and regions.

- Create banking-regulations requiring all government-reserve protected banks to give higher loan-rating points and lower interest-rates for businesses or projects that provide current or long-term benefits to the environment or to human well-being, while giving lower loan-rating points and higher interest-rates to those businesses or projects that have negative long-term effects on the environment or to human well-being.

- In order to determine the approval-ranking of a proposed loan, as compared with other proposed loans, each proposed loan is given higher or lower loan-rating points, depending on a ratio of its environmental, human and future Benefits compared to its environmental, human and future Costs. This loan-qualifying ratio and its correlated loan-rating points can also determine the offered interest-rate for each proposed loan, in which a higher benefits-to-costs ratio determines a lower interest-rate, while a lower benefits-to-costs ratio determines a higher interest-rate.

Economic Penalties for Environmental Harms

*Business fines or tax-penalties
for damages to ecosystems or the climate*

– Governments need to establish protective laws, fines, and special taxes to make businesses financially accountable for business activities that directly or indirectly cause harmful consequences to the environment, natural resources, ecosystems or climate.

– Environmental Costs (including ecological and climate-change costs, waste-disposal costs, and resource-depletion costs), due to business activities or products, must be internalized into the business' profit/costs accounting, and these environmental costs should be paid to the government or to the affected communities.

– Internalize into the selling price, the full environmental costs of sold products; thus influencing purchasing & consumption to shift towards environmentally-beneficial products.

– Climate-harming costs from carbon emissions can be paid by carbon-taxes, emission-penalties, or by a required purchasing of carbon-credits in a government directed cap-and-trade market.

Economic Incentives for Environmental Improvements

Business tax-reductions, rebates, subsidies, or gov contracts for improving ecosystems or reducing climate-change

– Incentivize clean and renewable energy production, clean fuels, clean energy technologies, and reliable energy infrastructure.

– Incentivize environmentally-sustainable production and consumption.

– Incentivize the development and available supply of environmentally-friendly and climate-helpful industrial technologies & consumer products.

– Incentivize the industrial use of emission-reducing and emission-capturing technologies.

– Incentivize the consumer use of environmentally-friendly and climate-helpful products.

– Incentivize the recycling and reuse of plastics, metals, and other non-degradable products, and incentivize local recycling collection systems, effective separation methods, and material-recycling businesses.

- Incentivize community projects and businesses that increase natural carbon-capture.

- Incentivize soil regeneration, organic farming, and local sustainable food production.

- Incentivize an increase, restoration, and stewardship of forests, wildlands, and nature reserves (public or private owned).

- Incentivize the ecological restoration, improvement and maintenance of coastal marine and wetland areas.

- Incentivize ocean cleanup and ocean carbon-capture projects.

- Incentivize corporate investments in natural carbon-capture projects, with tax-breaks & carbon-offset credits.

- Incentivize banks to help fund, with low-interest loans, community projects and businesses that help mitigate or reverse climate-change, improve the farming soil, or improve the local ecosystems.

- Incentivize banks to help fund, with low-interest loans, community projects and businesses that provide a needed service or benefit to a community or to the larger society.

4
Teaching Social
& Ecological Values

Teach Social & Ecological Values through education and global media

– Governments and educational institutions can encourage and teach peaceful social values and environmental values.

– Teach social & ecological values that support the long-term health & flourishing of human communities and ecological systems.

– Educate through global media to raise awareness of ecological problems and social problems needing to be solved.

– In colleges/universities teach a model of economics and business, in which broad social & environmental benefits are the Central-Priority Goals; rather than profit and wealth-accumulation for those companies or investment groups.

Teach Social Values

– Teach basic human rights and respect for personal freedoms, without prejudice or discrimination towards any gender, race, ethnic, religious, cultural, or political groups.

– Teach respect for the inherent dignity of all human beings, including their physical & emotional needs and their intellectual & creative potentials.

– Teach children to treat all people with respect, care and consideration, without prejudice against any gender, race, ethnicity, religion or culture.

– Teach the social value of nonviolence, compassion, caring, and cooperation.

– Teach the ideal of peaceful communities and social relations.

– Teach peaceful methods for resolving social conflicts and disputes.

– Teach children self-responsibility and encourage them to help others.

– Teach young men to treat women with personal respect and protect them from sexual abuse.

– Teach the value of family planning and methods of natural birth control, to help with maintaining a sustainable local population.

– Offer knowledge of various moral and spiritual teachings from worldwide cultures.

– Encourage the development & unfoldment of each person's human potentials & talents.

Teach Environmental Values

– Recognize life's interrelatedness and interdependency.

– Respect the Earth and the diversity of life

– Acknowledge the need for environmental-ecological caring and stewardship.

– Consider the environmental needs of future generations in all present decisions & actions.

– Teach the knowledge and skills needed for an ecologically-sustainable way of life.

– Learn from traditional indigenous knowledge about how to sustainably live in cooperation with the local natural ecology.

– Teach ecological sciences and ecological sustainability, and the practical knowledge for ecological sustainability.

– Teach respect and protection of special places of natural, cultural and spiritual significance.

– Teach and encourage an ethical non-cruel treatment of animals in animal-food farming and in science experiments.

Teach a Global Perspective

– encourage students to think about and envision the future, along with creative solutions for global problems

– affirm each student's capacity to shape the future

– teach how all people are interconnected in many ways

– teach how global problems and issues are interrelated

– teach concern for all people and the whole planet

– teach about the difficulties of many people & regions

– teach to see from the perspective of different people

– teach respect for cultural diversity and ethnic heritage

– teach how people affect the local and global environment

– teach how people are affected by their environment

– teach stewardship of the Earth, ecology, land, water, and air

– teach indigenous cultural attitudes of respecting and caring for nature

– teach the principles of human rights and the need to protect people's safety

– teach about the essential needs of all people everywhere globally

Teach Humanity's Shared Needs & Values

Teach the Values of:

– International Peacebuilding, Diplomacy, and Cooperation

– Non-violence, Safe Communities, and Peaceful Relations

– Human Rights and Civil Freedoms

– Fair Economics and Equal Opportunities

– Healthcare and Education for Everyone

– Nutritious Food, Clean Water, and Safe Shelter

– Environmental & Climate Protection

– Preserving Biodiversity & Wildlife

The Goals & Activities of the United Nations

Five focus areas of the UN

Peacemaking & Peacebuilding

Global Human Rights

Global Education

Global Health & Clean Water

Global Ecology & Climate

Promote & Protect Human Rights

Solve international conflicts
Peacefully & Nonviolently

Make International Peace Treaties
& use Peacekeeping Operations

Assist with Peacebuilding
& Post-conflict Restoration

Promote Peace & Nonviolence
in schools & communities

Reduce & gradually eliminate
mass-destructive weapons

Protect Human Rights
& Civil Freedoms

Investigate political detentions
& unjust imprisonment

Promote Fair Justice
& Equal Opportunities

Protect Labour Safety
& Promote Fair-payed work

Facilitate Fair Trade Contracts
& Advise trade cooperatives

Ensure access to New Technologies
technical-info & know-how

Promote Equal Opportunities
to participate in government

Open Opportunities to Participate
in UN conferences & proposals

Promote Human Values
through media & education

Promote & Protect Sustainable Ecosystems

Protect the Planetary Ecosystems,
biodiversity, wildlife & habitats

Protect the existing Forests
& freshwater ecosystems

Conserve 30% of the Earth's
land and sea by 2030

Promote Sustainable Management
& regeneration of living ecosystems

Ensure the Sustainable Use
of land & ocean resources

Protect Ocean Ecosystems
by Ecological Laws of the Sea

Reduce Global Warming
& Climate Change

Protect Local Environments
from pollution of air, water & land

Require Businesses to pay
for their Environmental Damages

Promote Ecological Values
through media & education

Promote Economic Generosity to improve the Lives of all People

Improve the Quality of Life
for people & communities

Increase Economic Generosity
from the wealthier to those in need

Eliminate Food Insecurity
Hunger & Malnutrition

Improve access to Clean Water
& sanitation facilities

Ensure People's Basic Needs,
good food, clean water, safe shelter

Improve access to Healthcare
& health counseling services

Deliver Humanitarian Assistance
& Emergency Aid

Improve Economic Development
& Infrastructure in poorer nations

Eliminate Extreme Poverty
& Economic Insecurity

Create Community-helpful
& Ecologically-helpful Jobs

Assist Local Businesses
that serve social & ecological needs

Improve access to Education
Life-skills & Job-skills

Promote Economic Investment for a Sustainable & Livable Planet

Invest in Ecological Restoration
& environmental improvements

Invest in Climate-solving projects
& emission-reduction technologies

Invest in Renewable Clean Energy
& non-polluting fuels

Invest in Recycling Processes
& energy-saving technologies

Invest in Locally-scaled
& Eco-friendly Industries

Invest in making urban areas
eco-sustainable & econ-resilient

Invest in Sustainable Agriculture
& regenerative soil improvement

Invest in Sustainable Forestry
& other natural carbon-collectors

Help poorer regions adapt to
climate-changes & severe weather

24 Sustainable Development Goals

(in 3 Categories)

Ecological-Environmental Goals

Clean Air & Fresh Water

Restoring Plant & Water Ecosystems

Restoring Forests & Farm Soils

Restoring Wildlife & Habitats

Restoring Oceans and Ocean Life

Beautifying Natural Environments

Mitigating Climate Change

Clean & Renewable Energy

Social-Economic Goals

Basic Needs: Food, Water, Shelter

Sanitation & Waste Disposal

Healthcare & Emergency Services

Quality Education & Skills Learning

Work Opportunities & Fair Wages

Civil Rights & Social Freedoms

Equal Laws & Fair Justice

Safe Communities & Protections

Sustainable-Economic Goals

Sustainable Local Economies

Sustainable Industry & Transportation

Sustainable Water & Energy Sources

Sustainable Farm & Food Systems

Adapting to Climate Change

Weather Preparedness & Resilience

Economic Agreements & Fair Trade

Public & Private Helpful Investments

4 General Guidelines for Sustainable Development

Economic development must be inclusive, equitable and accessible for all people, all genders, races, ethnic and cultural groups, and it must not violate people's human rights and civil liberties.

Economic development should not accelerate economic inequalities, nor should it primarily benefit corporations, investors, speculators, or contractors.

Economic development must be ecologically sustainable into the long-term future, and it should improve the natural resources of that bio-region, rather than harm or deplete those natural resources.

Economic development will depend on the local/regional ecosystems and resources, sustainable energy sources, water supply and farm soil.

Sustainable Development Objectives

Sustainable-Ecological needs

Protect, restore, improve and sustain
local ecosystems, natural environments,
habitats, wildlife, and biodiversity.

Protect and restore fresh water sources,
rivers, wetlands, and natural springs.

Protect and restore farm soil, forests,
wildlands and natural reserves.

Protect and restore the oceans, bays,
coastal flora, coral reefs, and ocean life.

Provide economic incentives to businesses
that restore local ecosystems,
and penalize businesses that harm ecosystems.

Provide financial help for the restoration,
regeneration, regreening and revegetation
of degraded or barren land.

Solve the global climate-change problem
by financially penalizing
carbon-emitting industries and products,
while incentivizing those that increase carbon-sequestration.

Develop and maintain eco-sustainable cities & communities,
with clean and renewable energy,
reliable & resilient infrastructure,
sustainable food and water systems,
and eco-responsible industries, products, and recycling.

Economic-Development needs

Improve the lives of everyone
with good food, clean water & safe shelter.

Improve local food systems,
food production and food availability.

Improve local water supplies
and water access.

Improve public facilities for sanitation,
hygiene, and proper waste-disposal.

Improve housing and safe shelter,
public spaces and parks.

Improve healthcare and educational services.

Improve the supply and affordability
of needed and desired products.

Improve economic infrastructure
and sustainable renewable energy supply.

Improve job training, work opportunities,
and decent livable wages.

Improve business opportunities
and accessible low-interest loans.

Improve local economic progress
and maximize local economic autonomy.

Improve regional economic trade
and regional collaborative projects.

Social Rights & Justice needs

Respect all people everywhere,
giving all people human rights and freedoms,
equal rights, fair justice, and equal votes,
without social or political discrimination.

Respect people's freedom and diversity
in beliefs, religion, culture, choices,
lifestyles, art and expression.

Protect people's security and safety,
with an atmosphere of nonviolence.

Promote political and social inclusiveness,
equal opportunities, worker rights and fair trade.

Help communities achieve:
equal civil rights and fair justice
safety and nonviolence
healthcare, child and elderly care
education and work-skills learning
local business opportunities
ecological responsibility

14 Environmental Goals for Governments

Protect & Restore ecosystems and biodiversity

Protect & Restore water & forest ecosystems

Protect Natural Resources from overuse & depletion

Protect Oceans & Bays from pollution & overfishing

Reduce Industrial Pollution of the air, water, and land

Protect Endangered Wildlife and preserve natural habitats

Establish Conservation Areas, wildlife & nature reserves

Protect Natural Beauty, scenic places & landscapes

Reduce Greenhouse Gases to reduce climate change

Produce & Use clean & renewable energies

Increase Recycling of products & materials

Improve Energy-efficiency in heating & cooling buildings

Increase Forests & Wetlands for natural carbon-capture

Improve Agricultural Soils & increase regenerative farming

What can all Nations agree on?

1. International Peace & Treaties

2. Helpful Economic Collaboration

3. Human Rights & Freedoms

4. Ensuring Food, Water, Shelter

5. Human Safety & Nonviolence

6. Healthcare & Medical Services

7. Education & Skills Learning

8. Available Jobs & Fair Pay

9. Fair Loans & Fair Trade

10. Protecting our Earth
    the natural ecologies and wildlife,
    the natural environment and climate,
    the natural beauty and scenic places.

www.ingramcontent.com/pod-product-compliance
Lightning Source LLC
Chambersburg PA
CBHW030450220526
45464CB00006B/2471